First Year Teacher Survival Guide
Pocket Edition

By Jessica Doering

A note from the author:

If you are a first-year teacher (or a teacher who struggled a lot your first year and still are looking for help and answers), this book is for you! I have written tips based on my own personal experiences and observations that I hope will enhance your preparation for your first year. I have personally read a lot about teaching and education and have learned that many books offer generic advice ("Organize your room efficiently") but don't offer specifics on how to follow their advice. I have created a list of ten mistakes to avoid, but have not just left you hanging…I give advice on what you should do instead! I share about strategies I have used, activities I have implemented, and attitudes I have taken on that I wish someone had told me before I started teaching. At the end of the book, you will find a beginning of the year checklist, beginning of the year activities, and a sample syllabus and parent letter for you to use as a guide.

I am sure there are dozens of great tips out there that I didn't discuss in this book. Feel free to email me and share your ideas on mistakes first-year teachers should avoid, and I can share them with others on my blog themrsdoering.wordpress.com. Email me at mrsjessicadoering@gmail.com and I would be delighted to read your ideas!

Thanks for reading!

Jessica Doering

Mistake #1: Trying to appear "cool" and laid back with your students to the detriment of classroom discipline.

It's the first day of school and you want to impress your students with your charm and friendly attitude. You smile a lot and skip the rules and syllabus for a first day full of "getting to know you games" and other fun activities. You want kids to like you because you think that they will respond to you more if you aren't strict. Big mistake.

While the "fun teachers" may be some of the most "liked" teachers in school, I consistently hear students say things like "I like Mr. ____ because we don't do anything in that class." or "Ms. ____ is the best. I just sit on my phone the whole class period and she lets us sleep when we want to." I hope you cringe when you hear these types of statements from students. And I hope you didn't get into teaching for approval and that you actually care about leaning. If you care about learning and student outcomes, I am going to let you in on a secret: learning happens within structured classrooms.

Take classroom rules seriously and enforce them when necessary. It's ok to be friendly but it isn't ok to be friends with students. Be funny or sweet or whatever it is that allows you to do you, but don't forget about the rules and discipline. I am assuming you didn't get into teaching to be well-liked by students and to have the approval of teenagers. This leads to unhealthy relationships and if you are going into teaching to be "the cool teacher," you should consider another profession.

Obviously, I am not suggesting you become a mean teacher that nobody likes, but valuing their approval over their understanding of the subject you teach is dangerous. Fun can absolutely happen within a structured classroom, and students respond better to a teacher who has their classroom under control.

What to do instead: The first day of school is their first impression of you. If you appear to be structured and have set rules and discipline, students are less likely to try to take advantage of you. Make the first day about your rules and expectations and incorporate students in the process. I have done several activities that kept the kids engaged and still allowed us to discuss the rules and expectations for my classroom. Below are some ideas for activities that you can use to structure your first few days which are the most vital days for establishing discipline and classroom procedures.

Activity #1: Create four posters, each one with one of these questions:

- What can Mr./Mrs._____ (teacher) do to help you be successful in this class?

- What can you do to help you be successful in this class?

- What can other students do to be successful in this class?

- Our classroom should be _____ every day.

Hand students four sticky notes when they come in the door. Ask them to fill out one sticky note to answer each of the questions and then ask them to stick their answers to the posters when they are finished with their responses. After you have given them time to answer and stick their notes on the posters, thank them for their responses and read several from each poster to the class.

Pro Tip: Make sure you give students a time limit. Otherwise, this will drag out forever. I also like to do this activity as they are coming in on the first day when I have a lot to pass out to them. It gives them something to do while we are setting up for the first day and keeps them quiet until I am ready to begin. I also always try to include at least one funny response from each poster and laugh with the kids. It is a real bonding moment.

Why does this activity work?

> Quite simply, telling students what you are going to do to help them or what they need to do to help themselves or how the classroom should be every day is not as powerful as hearing the responses from other students. This activity usually results in honest, mature answers that will mimic the types of responses you would give yourself, but the kids love hearing it from each other.
>
> This exercise showed students that it is not just important to me that there is order in the classroom, but that their peers value rules and expectations. Plenty of responses from students emphasized the need for a quiet classroom, mutual respect, help from peers when they struggle, and for other students to adhere to the rules. Way better than it coming from my mouth--the kids respond better to other kids and value what they say a lot.

Activity #2: Put students into groups and assign each group a classroom rule from the syllabus. Give each group a poster and some markers. Have each group make a poster with the rule written at the top and a "looks like/sounds like chart" in the middle that says what it "looks like" to follow that rule and what it "sounds like" to follow that rule. Lastly, ask them to write a list at the bottom of possible consequences they feel would be appropriate for not following the rule.

To the right is an example of what a poster could look like. (This one is a mini-poster made with just a small piece of paper.)

After the time you have given them to complete the activity is up, have one person from each group go to the board to share the poster with the class. Have them read each part to everyone.

Why does this activity work?

This activity works because it allows you to create the boundaries for your classroom without completely taking the students' out of the process for creating rules and expectations. Students feel involved, and they often give much more harsh punishments than you would for the same offense. This activity is also fun for creative students and gets students working in groups the first week of school.

Pro Tip: This is a great activity to do to establish your group work routines. Always start the year with explicit rules for their behavior when they are getting to their group, while working in the group, and when they are supposed to return to their seats. I also always give them time limits for each task. For example, "You have 10 seconds to move to your group, be seated with them, and be silently waiting for instruction." Or "Your group has 15 minutes to complete your poster. If you would like to have a piece of paper to sketch out your poster, have one person from your group come up to the table and get a piece." Make sure they know their expectations for this time.

See Appendix B for more information about these two activities.

Mistake #2: Not keeping up with grading each week (and trying to grade every assignment).

My biggest weakness as a teacher is keeping up with grading. Don't get me wrong, I am organized and have all of it ready to grade. I even take papers home every night to grade them. The problem is that I have no motivation to do it in the evenings and it piles up until I have a deadline to get grades in. Then I am grading like 10 assignments in one night and am up until 3am putting grades in because they are supposed to be posted by 8am. I don't recommend this approach for several reasons. First, you will feel better if you stay on top of your grades. You will have relief when you have nothing to grade on the weekend (more on how to accomplish this later) and you will have less stress when it comes time to post grades for report cards. My school has a rule that grades should be updated every Friday, but I got too overwhelmed to get it in by then. I learned my lesson on this one. Don't let grades pile up.

Also, do NOT grade everything they ever do. It is overwhelming and you will be in possession of thousands of papers a week. Don't do it. It is ok to give them a practice worksheet just for the sake of them practicing. If you are circulating throughout the classroom and you know the students are all working and have made progress, don't feel obligated to collect the papers for a grade. And just because you collect the paper doesn't mean you have to grade it. You can look through to find common errors and have students correct their own work the following day. Make things as easy on yourself as possible when it comes to grading because you will always be behind and I promise you will never feel caught up.

<u>What you should do instead:</u> Make a rule that everything you need to grade each week has to be graded by Friday afternoon (or if you are super diligent about the use of your planning period, you can make a rule that all daily work and small quizzes are graded before you leave for the day). Give yourself grace if you fall a little behind, but make that the exception to your rule. Pick a rule for yourself and stick with it. I mean it.

The other huge tip I have is to utilize peer-grading. I would have students switch papers and grade each other's work whenever possible. This was awesome because students could see how they did and I could choose to take it for an official grade without having to do all of the work. I even allow students to grade their own papers occasionally and this saves me so much time! Do whatever you can to minimize the time you spend checking easy answers. Create assignments that are easy to grade and you can check over quickly if you are going to grade it yourself.

<u>Pro Tip:</u> The best advice? If you are super overwhelmed and you have small formative assignments (warm-ups, exit slips, etc.) that the kids have already forgotten about, throw them out (recycle if possible). And don't feel guilty.

Mistake #3: Not utilizing your planning period for grading and copies.

I am an introvert and I need a break sometimes during the day just to decompress. I will eat, surf the Internet, play games, or talk with my teacher friend. And sometimes you need this majorly, and it's ok to take some "me time" if you need it. But the rule for yourself should be productivity during your planning. I wasted hours I could have been grading and copying, and those tasks I had to do didn't go away. Instead, I was copying after school until 5pm and grading papers at home instead of cooking dinner for my husband. I didn't have a plan for most of my weeks for this time during the day and without planning out what to do, I wasted time. Time is money. Don't waste it.

What to do instead: Make a plan for each day as to what you need to grade and copy during planning (and don't forget about parent meetings and other mandatory meetings they will schedule during your planning, too) and then make sure you accomplish these tasks. Give yourself one day a week that is flexible so if you get behind or spend the hour chatting with a friend, you will be able to still accomplish everything for the week without getting behind. Again, don't beat yourself up if you aren't productive, but if you make a habit of not being productive, you will ultimately spend way more time outside of school grading and doing other boring tasks.

Pro tip: Do whatever works for you to keep you organized. Don't worry about following another teacher's organization methods, but do steal their organizational ideas when they work for you! Watch what other teachers do and try it out. Use sticky notes, to-do lists, reminders in your phone, a planner, etc. if it helps. Don't use them if they don't. And don't spend too much time organizing yourself to the detriment of actually getting things done! Sometimes, I would spend more time organizing myself than I would spend on the actual tasks at hand, and that's because I love to make lists and charts and organize things. I just don't love to make copies or grade quizzes or be productive.

Mistake #4: Thinking you can change everything that is wrong about this profession.

There are many things about this profession that suck. Many kids don't care about what you are teaching and this won't change no matter how "engaging" your lessons are. Research shows that there is actually little you can do to make a child successful if their home life is not good and their parents aren't interested in their life. The "difference" teachers make is not usually seen right away, so if you want to "make a difference" and that's your only motivation for teaching, there are other professions that will lead to more obvious, short-term, tangible change. Administrators aren't out to back you up unless they can do it without risking their own butts (which many districts make it impossible to do because they have administrators trained to be compliant with all district-level requests or risk their job). Innovations fail and are replaced with other innovations and before you know it, there is another innovation that will supposedly change everything. (Don't believe them.) When an innovation comes along that will truly be the best thing for students, there will be push back from teachers and administrators because they don't want to change or it will be too hard or whatever excuse you can think of. You will be asked to do more with less every year and you don't get paid enough to do it. While not every teacher faces the same struggles and each district has its own quirks, there will definitely be things you hate and you can't do much about any of it. Something unfair? Deal with it. Something ridiculous (like being asked to submit the same thing in two different and equally annoying district websites)? So what? This is education. Whatever is fair or right makes the most sense, we do the opposite. Get used to it.

<u>What to do instead:</u> There are occasionally times when you can actually do something to improve your profession and

when they come along, do them. Join a committee or read the most recent articles on education and stay connected to the university nearby (because they have cool ideas and the money to blow on researching innovations). Do what you can. And have a teacher friend who understands your frustrations and will listen to you complain without judgment. Honestly, teacher friends understand your pain and will be more willing to talk about it for lengthy periods of time than your spouse or friend. Nobody else will understand fully all of the crap you deal with better than your best teacher friends.

PRO TIP: Make sure you are only talking to someone you trust when venting about school issues. People will talk about you, and if word gets back to the administration about your complaints, you could be reprimanded. By the time it reaches the principal, who knows how twisted your words will be? Just stick with trusted friends who understand and share your feelings. When in doubt about if you should share with someone, ask "If the principal was listening, would I say this?" If the answer is that you wouldn't say it in front of administration, refrain from saying it.

Mistake #5: Trying to do every neat teacher trick you learned about in your education classes in college or you read about in the latest education journal.

Colleges are teaching the newest, coolest innovations and tricks that you can find out there because they have the money to do research and hundreds of teachers at their disposal to practice and experiment with. You will no doubt have learned that there are tons of ways you can improve your classroom and if you are like me and you read a lot of education books and articles, you will be overwhelmed with all of the things you could or should be doing to improve your classroom. You will want to do a hundred different little things based on what you have learned (tips for organizing, for grading, for discipline, for setting up your room, for helping "problem students" to be successful, etc.) but you can't do it all. You simply can't. You will wear yourself out and end up only doing things half way. Trust me, I have tried to do it. You can't. I am NOT saying you can't do lots of things to help your classroom run smoothly. However, I am saying that these big, time-consuming, cool innovations that you think will make a huge difference cannot all be done in one year. You need to focus on the basics and then find a few innovative theories you want to try to test out in your classroom. Don't try to do all of them at one time.

Tip for avoiding this mistake: Make a list of all of the cool things you want to do in your classroom and all of the tips you have. (If you are thinking "What is she talking about?! I don't have a hundred things I want to do in my classroom." then maybe you should start reading up in education journals or books or articles because people are doing some really cool things and you are missing out!) Think about what will make the biggest impact for your students and circle the top six things you will want to do. Then, think about what will help you the most in your efficiency and put a star by the top four. Lastly, think about these ten tips and which tips you need to have in place at the beginning of the year and what can wait. If it has to be in place at the beginning of the year, make it the biggest priority. Put them in order of priority and make those ten ideas happen. (For a list of changes I made in my classroom that made a difference, read my book *10 Small Classroom Changes That Make a Huge Impact*.)

If there are any tips or tricks that don't require you to do things on an ongoing basis, think about implementing them at the beginning of the year and then seeing how they work. Like that new way teachers are organizing their desks? Try it. Like the memes people are displaying to teach kids the rules? Try it. As long as it is something that is easy to do, doesn't require you to constantly upkeep it, and is something you can easily change if it doesn't work, try it out. The changes you want to avoid making a lot of at one time are big changes that may require a lot of maintenance on your part to make them work.

Let it go that you can't do everything. It's ok. See what works the first semester (or trimester if your school is into that kind of thing) and if something didn't work, scrap or revise the idea. If it did, keep it. If you feel like you can take on another challenge, go back to the list and see what you can incorporate.

Pro Tip: Not all ideas can be implemented half way through the year. Make sure you are making changes that are consistent with your rules and classroom procedures. If it doesn't fit but you love it, file it away and revisit for next year.

Mistake #6: Ignoring sound advice from veteran teachers and being a first-year know-it-all.

There is plenty of advice that you will get that sucks or just simply doesn't work for you and your classroom. But listening to teachers who have been at it for a while will save you time and energy. I didn't really fall into this trap myself, but I know that many first-year teachers can think that they are more knowledgeable than veteran teachers because they have access to and knowledge about the newest technology and research and resources they learned about in school. And there is some truth to the fact that veteran teachers can be unwilling to look into or think about new ideas because they feel like they have seen it all and they know what works. BUT they also have thousands more classroom hours than you and have so much wisdom.

What to do instead: Seek the advice of veteran teachers when you need help or when you are having a rough time. They are also great resources for when you need something and they usually have the answers when you have questions (*Where are those copy work orders again? Who should I talk to about maternity leave paperwork?*). I learned a lot from my supervising teacher during student teaching about organization, classroom set up, how to check homework efficiently, and how to keep track of which grades you have put into the grade book. She reminded me to walk around the room and have students go to the board whenever possible and to keep binders containing the materials I used with their answer keys so I didn't have to redo everything each year. She gave me so many small tips and I learned so much by watching her that I am not sure what I would do if it wasn't for her advice. Watch veteran teachers, learn from their advice, and don't think you know more than them.

Sometimes, you will be annoyed with teachers who resist change or want to do things in a way that you might feel is inefficient. The thing to remember is that they have been through many changes over the years they have taught, and they know that most of the changes that are made in education go almost as quickly as they come. This means that they might be more resistant to changes that you think are really great, and it is reasonable for them to feel this way. Don't be upset with them about this, but instead, listen to why they are resistant to change, and find compromises when possible.

Pro Tip: There are times when you should consider deferring to the veteran teacher, even when you know that what you want to do might be better or more efficient. Some fights aren't worth fighting.

Mistake #7: Not learning names fast enough.

Kids want to know care about them. They want to know you are paying attention and that you are genuinely interested in getting to know them. If they feel like you care, they will warm up more quickly, be more willing to work hard, and feel like a part of the classroom. If you don't know their names, there are a lot of issues this causes. (This is important for all teachers, but especially teachers who have a lot of kids every day because you have more names to learn.)

First, discipline becomes an issue. Picture this: a kid is talking during class across the room from where you are and you want to ask them to be quiet but you don't know their name. Or a student is running through the hallways on the way to lunch and you want to tell them to slow down and chill out but you don't know their name. Or think of any other disciplinary situation you can imagine and you have no idea what the child's name is. I promise this is a huge problem. Kids act out all of the time and sometimes you can't give nonverbal directions to them because they can't see you, you are too far from them, or they don't know it is directed at them. These are times when saying their name might actually be all it takes to redirect them to appropriate behavior.

The second issue that is brought up is that you can't call on them individually to check for understanding and know how much certain kids know if you don't know their name. A lot of teachers don't prioritize this, including retiring teachers who are "on the way out" and newbie teachers who don't understand the importance. Don't be one of them.

What to do instead: Do whatever it takes to memorize their names. There are so many tricks. What works for me is to spend ten minutes going through the classroom and asking them to tell me their name. I repeat it back to them and then try to memorize one row at a time. When I have one row memorized, I move on to the next row and then try to say both rows. Some people might think this is wasted instructional time, but it doesn't take much time, the kids like to see if you can memorize all of their names in one class period (I haven't been successful at it yet, but I have gotten very close to having all 150-ish names memorized in one day and I have all of them memorized by the end of the first three days of school).

Play name games, make them wear name tags, come up with pneumonic devices, have them make name cards to put on their desk, make connections to people you know with the same name (kid named Michael is easy to remember because that's my dad's name, kid named Bradley is easy because that's my husband's name, etc.). Whatever it takes, make learning their names a priority. Seating charts are a must for this and we will talk about this further in the next tip.

Mistake #8: Letting kids sit wherever they want.

This mistake leads to a lot of problems. First, like I have stated before, learning names is a high priority. You can't learn names as easily if they sit wherever they want every day. Some people think the independence they have from choosing their seat is good for kids, but in my experience, even high school kids expect a seating chart and they are better behaved when they are in one. Some people take the "pick your seat the first day and that's your seat" approach, but your number one ally in classroom management is a teacher-directed seating chart. Students will choose to sit by friends and will talk more often if you let them choose their seat. If you don't give them a seating chart the first day, it will make it more difficult to enforce seating charts later when you realize that they are nuts and will not stop talking because you let them choose where to sit. They will question you as to why you changed your mind. Trust me--seating charts are amazing and getting them just right takes time.

What to do instead: Start with an alphabetical seating chart. Kids are used to this and you can learn their names easily. It doesn't matter if it's left to right, right to left, front of the row to back of the row, or whatever. I just always start alphabetically. This makes it easier to pass back papers as you learn their names. Have a seating chart handy at your desk (more amazing organizational tips in my book *10 Quick Tips for Organizing Your Classroom*) and refer to it as you learn their names. When you change their seats throughout the year, be conscious of IEPs and 504s that require preferential seating, and make sure you place friends who talk away from each other. Don't be afraid to move kids half way through a class if the talking will not stop. I had a lot of talkers in one class and it was almost impossible to find a seating chart that worked.

When I did, I kept them in those seats for the remainder of the year.

Note: If you fall into the "no seating chart camp" because you want them to have independence, remember that there will be plenty of other opportunities for this throughout the year, including activities during which time students can choose their partner or seat. Trust me on this one. Please. Give them a seating chart. It will be worth it.

Mistake #9: Planning really far in advance and not being flexible.

It's ok to plan things in advance and to have an idea of what you want to do. Obviously. But I have learned that you may think something is going to happen one way and the lesson takes ten times as long as you thought or you couldn't get through along the notes because you were answering good questions about the content or your kids need more practice than you realized. Whatever it is that comes up, you need to be flexible. If you have a plan for the first month of school already down to the assignments you will give and the homework problems you will assign, you are probably forgetting that the kids will have different needs and will "interfere" with your plans (and I mean that in the best possible way). They are unique and you will have to be flexible. Otherwise, you will force them to do activities that either a) they are not ready for or b) they are too advanced to do. Boo that.

What to do instead: Have a general plan of action and pick great activities and problems. But don't do an activity if your kids have shown they have a good understanding and don't need it, or if it is too advanced for where they are at the moment. Be flexible in the problems you will assign because you don't know what they will be good at or bad at yet. I recommend not planning more than a week out for anything more specific than the general curriculum map. Activities and homework are best chosen once you have a good grasp of the level of understanding of your students.

I would make a list of all of the notes, activities, and assessments I wanted to give, and then put them in order for how I thought they could fit together. Then, I would make plans to go down the list in order, making sure to have copies of worksheets ready a few days in advance. Then, if students moved more quickly than I expected, I would have everything already prepared. If they moved more slowly than I expected, I would just shift everything back. Flexibility is key should be your motto. You need to be able to adapt to snow days, unexpected pep rallies for winning a state championship, family emergencies, the flu hitting your school and wiping out half of your class, etc.

Pro Tip: However you organize your lesson plans, it is very important to record what *actually* happened each day. I always left room in my planner under the lesson plan for the day to make a note of how far we got in the lesson, any big changes I made, and what homework I actually assigned that day. I would jot down these changes after each class period, and if one of my classes was further than another, it helped me to stay on track!

Mistake #10: Not having emergency sub plans ready.

The stomach bug will hit you when you are in the middle of a unit or your kid will get sick the day before a test. Having nothing prepared in case of an emergency sub day will leave you with two choices. You can either have nothing and make the office ladies mad at you because they will have to coordinate printing rosters and getting an assignment from your colleague to copy, or you can work from home at 6am trying to piece together plans and emailing your teacher friend a list of tasks you will beg them to do for you that morning. Either way, you and your students lose.

What to do instead: Have a folder with emergency sub plans together. Make it easily accessible (some schools keep it in a central location in the office, but yours might just have you keep it in your room).

Your emergency sub plan folder should contain:

- Rosters for all classes (and seating charts if you have them-- which you should)

- Instructions for any activities you are planning, a list of "trusted students" they can ask if they need anything (only pick kids who are legit and will not lie to the sub--think teacher's pet types).

- Copies of a content-related assignment (practice standardized tests or review worksheets for previously-learned but commonly misunderstood works well for me).

- Instructions for what to collect (I always recommend you have them collect everything or the kids have no incentive to do the activity during class).

- Specific instructions for where to leave any collected assignments.

- A big thank you for the sub who is coming into your classroom. These subs are walking into the unknown when they come into your room and their job is often thankless. Think of them when you are making the plans.

In general, all sub plans should always be detailed and include where all classes are located (if you have any outside of your main classroom or if you are a floating teacher), any extra duties you have (hall duty, cafeteria duty, etc.), and the order in which you want the activities to be done. Once I reach the point in the year when they are doing things without me asking (like starting their warmup or putting papers in their bin when finished), I tell the sub what the kids should do and I expect my students to do what they should do without being asked.

There you have it! Ten mistakes to avoid your first year of teaching! Remember, teaching is hard, and you will get burnt out quickly if you don't find an outlet for your frustrations. I recommend writing a blog, talking to a teacher friend, watching teacher humor videos online, reading about innovations in education (helps you remember that there is more to your job than just babysitting), or laughing at teacher memes. Breathe, be organized and prepared, and remember that the kids who are the hardest to love are often the ones who need it the most. Good luck with your first year! Feel free to reach out to me at mrsjessicadoering@gmail.com if you become overwhelmed and need some help! I would be happy to help if I can!

Appendix A: Beginning of the Year Checklist

Whether this is your first year teaching or you have been doing it for thirty years, this checklist can help guide you to what you might need to do the first week of school, and offer suggestions for how to stay organized! It is always better to start the year off on the right foot with an organized, well-managed classroom than to try and catch up on organization later (hint: you will never catch up!).

To-Do List:

- ☐ Create a syllabus and accompanying parent letter (I have included a template/example for you in this packet!). You will need to clearly (but concisely) explain:
    - ○ General classroom rules and expectations
    - ○ Materials students need to bring daily to class
    - ○ Late work policy
    - ○ Attendance policy
    - ○ Grading scale for your class
    - ○ Cheating/plagiarism policy
- ☐ Decide how you want students to turn in work and where you will keep the papers once they are turned in. Then, organize your classroom accordingly.
    - ○ I always had small baskets (I bought mine at Target in the dollar section) for students to turn in their assignments, and placed these baskets on a table by the door (out of the way, but easily accessed as students come in the room). When students needed to turn in assignments, this is where they would go. This kept my desk clear of clutter, and I could get the assignments out of the baskets and organize them before they ever went on my desk or in my bag.
    - ○ I also had an accordion file for late assignments. I liked to keep these separate from the other

assignments since loose papers tend to get lost more easily.

- ☐ Decide how students will access papers they did not receive because they were absent and organize your room accordingly!
    - o I had binders with clear page protectors in them and would slip all extra worksheets into a page protector at the end of class. Students who were absent or lost their assignment could go to the binder and get what they needed without having to come to me.
- ☐ Decide procedures for the important tasks your students will be completing. Make sure you have clear expectations for these times, including volume level, when students should begin the activity, what your expectations are once they are working, etc. Be sure to establish those expectations the first, second, and even third time you ask students to complete the task. Then, remind students as needed throughout the year. Here are some suggestions for the tasks you should develop expectations for:
    - o Warm-ups
    - o Getting into groups
    - o Turning in homework
    - o Turning in late work
    - o Going to the bathroom/leaving the room (Sign out sheet? Hall pass?)
    - o How to establish they have a question or are having trouble understanding (raising hand, calling out, using a green/yellow/red system for establishing their level of understanding, etc.)
- ☐ Set up your students' desks in the arrangement that will be most often used in your classroom.
    - o All students facing the front is useful for a lecture-style classroom with little chance for distractions. It is good in an environment in which you need to keep control over the classroom and students are most often working independently.

- Everyone facing the middle of the room (two sections of desks facing each other) is a good set-up for discussion-based classes where it is good for students to see each other. The biggest downside to this setup is that students are easily distracted by the students on the other side of the room.
- Desks arranged in groups works well for classes that emphasize group work and collaboration. If you often have students working in partners and/or groups, discussing assignments with a neighbor, in tutoring groups, or other collaborative activities, then think about having this setup. I used this my third year of teaching and I loved it. The downside? Cheating is easier in this setup, but you can combat this. Have students set up folders to block other students from viewing their work during quizzes, and arrange the desks in rows facing the front for exams.
- Combining students facing the front with students in groups, putting students in rows facing the front with two rows put together in partners gives you the best of both worlds. Unfortunately, many traditional desks (ones with the desk and chair not separated) makes this setup difficult since students can't easily get in and out of the desks.

☐ Decide on a plan for the first week of classes.
- First day activities, follow-up activities in the days to follow
- Inevitable fire drill (make sure you have everything you need for this handy and ready to go!)
- Will you jump right in with new content, or will you do some review?
- Getting to know you games and activities—learning student names is ESSENTIAL for building relationships and for discipline!

☐ Organize your teacher planner. Put dates in if it doesn't have dates already, and write in your plans for the first week (or two!). Just know that your plans will likely have to change, so using pencil works well. I also knew teachers who would use the lesson planner that the school gave them, but use small post-it notes to write in the daily activities. Then, when a delay occurred (snow day, lockdown, early dismissal, unplanned assembly, etc.), they could just shift the post-it notes instead of rewriting their entire agenda.

- o Write in school holidays, meetings set for the first few weeks, dates for faculty meetings, parent-teacher conferences, etc.
- o Make sure you leave space for writing in the "actual" lesson—any changes from your planned lesson should be jotted down so that you remember them later. Didn't get to page 7? Write it. Passed out the assignment for tomorrow since you finished the lesson early? Write it!

☐ Make copies of everything you will need for the first week of school. Choose a time to do this when not many people are around. Don't be a copier hog, and don't get behind one in line either.

☐ Hang up posters and classroom expectations. Make the room feel welcoming, warm, and happy. Leave room for student work—you will want to display what students are creating on a regular basis!

☐ Create a sub folder with classroom rosters, procedures, your schedule, any assigned duties you have during the day, and lunch times. Have at least TWO emergency sub plan lessons put in the folder in case you are out unexpectedly for a few days. Some schools have a folder they want you to use for this, but if not, I recommend creating a binder. Be sure to include any pertinent instructions for students with allergies, special needs that will possibly need to be addressed by the substitute, and any additional student-specific information that might be helpful (Examples: John sometimes needs to take a break and go in the hallway to calm down for a few minutes—he is allowed to get up and go whenever he needs to. Susan uses a red card and can go to the office when she is feeling overwhelmed—if she shows you the card, let her go.). At this point, you might not know these things about your kids, but make sure you are updating the folder as the year goes on.

☐ Print rosters the day before school starts, or the morning of the first day of school. Rosters change often leading up to (and after) the start of school, so don't print them too early. Use these rosters for attendance for the first few days of school. Be sure to check every morning to see if any updates have been made to your roster. If you want to use an attendance book to write down student scores or take attendance, I recommend waiting until the end of the second week of classes to write their names into the attendance book because there are simply too many roster changes before this in most schools.

Appendix B: Beginning of the Year Activities

Post-It Posters:

This activity gives students the opportunity to express their needs and expectations for the classroom in an anonymous and simple way.

Materials Needed:

- Four poster boards
- Post-It Notes (I chose to get off-brand small ones at the dollar store)
    - You need enough for all of your students to have four post-its.
    - If they are too big, you won't be able to fit them all on the posters.

Preparation for the activity:

- Create four posters with the following questions/statements on them: (Make sure that the questions are written large enough for students to read from their desks.)
    - What should you do to help yourself to be successful in this class?
    - What should other students do to help you to be successful in this class?
    - Our classroom should be _____ every day.
    - What should the teacher do to help you to be successful in this class?
- Hang up the four posters on the board at the front of the class.
- Write instructions on the board before students come in the room. This way you don't have to verbally give instructions

and students can get started on the assignment before the bell rings! Here is what I wrote:

- o Directions for Post-It Activity:
  Please get 4 Post-Its and answer the questions (one on each post-it!). When you have answered all four questions, please put your post-its on the posters!

Lesson Plan:

- Have students working on the assignment as they walk in the door. This will cut down on the class time used for instructions and students getting supplies.
- Give students adequate time to write their answers and put the post-its on the board. I recommend that you give about 5-7 minutes total.
- Walk around to ensure that students are all answering the questions on the post-its and that they put their answers on the board.
- After the students have their answers on the board, thank them for their responses! At this point, you have some choices for how to proceed.
  - o I always told students that we would read and discuss these the next day. This allowed me to go over the syllabus and do other first-day activities, gave me time to read their responses and reflect on how to lead the discussion on the answers, and also provided a great way to start the second day (I would lead in with this and then do the Rules Charts with my students—starts them thinking about what they want the classroom to be like and then lets them put those ideas into practical terms!).
  - o If you prefer, you can read these out loud to your students and discuss them with the class after they are finished with the activity. Leading this discussion needs to be about affirming their needs in the classroom and giving them confirmation that you will

be trying to meet their expectations as they are trying to meet yours.

- o Another option would be to have students volunteer to share their answers to the questions in groups, then have a classroom discussion about those that stood out.

- If you want, you can easily leave these up on the walls in the classroom for a while as a reminder of their own expectations for themselves and the expectations that their peers have of them. TIP: If you use pretty post-its, it makes it even more pleasing to the eye and a better option to hang in the classroom!

Rules Charts:

However rules are decided upon in your classroom (whether you as the teacher make them or you allow more student input in creating the rules), this activity brings students into the process in a meaningful way.

Materials Needed:

- Papers or posters for the students to make their chart in groups.
- Markers

Preparation for the Activity:

- It helps to put students into groups in advance. I recommend no more than four people in a group.

Lesson Plan:

- Put students into groups and assign each group a classroom rule from the syllabus. Give each group a poster and some markers. Have each group make a poster with the rule written at the top and a "looks like/sounds like chart" in the middle that says what it "looks like" to follow that rule and what it "sounds like" to follow that rule. Lastly, ask them to write a list at the bottom of possible consequences they feel would be appropriate for not following the rule.
- After the time you have given them to complete the activity is up, have one person from each group go to the board to share the poster with the class. Have them read each part to everyone.
  - To the right is an example of what a poster could look like. (This one is a mini-poster made with just a small piece of paper.)

Why does this activity work?

This activity works because it allows you to create the boundaries for your classroom without completely taking the students' out of the process for creating rules and expectations. Students feel involved, and they often give much more harsh punishments than you would for the same offense. This activity is also fun for creative students and gets students working in groups the first week of school.

Pro Tip: This is a great activity to do to establish your group work routines. Always start the year with explicit rules for their behavior when they are getting to their group, while working in the group, and when they are supposed to return to their seats. I also always give them time limits for each task. For example, "You have 10 seconds to move to your group, be seated with them, and be silently waiting for instruction." Or "Your group has 15 minutes to complete your poster. If you would like to have a piece of paper to sketch out your poster, have one person from your group come up to the table and get a piece." Make sure they know their expectations for this time.

Beginning of the Year Survey (Can be adapted for your subject area!):

Before engaging in activities that are related to why your subject area is important or what your subject is all about, please consider having your students take a survey about their beliefs about your content area. I included in mine a few other questions that help me to gage student needs in the classroom, but that is obviously optional! The fun thing about this survey is that you can have students do it again later in the year and see how their responses have changed based on what they have learned in your classroom!

Materials Needed:

- Copies of the survey (on the next page) for all of your students.

Preparation for the Activity:

- Other than printing the copies, no other preparation needed!

Lesson Plan:

- This is a great warm-up activity to complete the first week of school. I encourage you to modify the survey to fit your students' needs.
- I gave students five minutes to complete the survey.
- An optional extension activity is to have students turn in their surveys and then discuss the questions one at a time in groups. You can ask follow-up questions such as:
    - o What do you think has influenced you to believe this way?
    - o What do you think it would take to change your mind about this?

- o If you strongly disagree or strongly agree with a statement, what makes your agreement or disagreement so strong? What has led you to such a strong opinion about this topic?
- EXTENSION: If you plan on having students answer these same questions later in the year, consider saving their responses and storing them away. Then have students retake the survey questions (the ones about their ideas about mathematics) and then show them their old responses. Lead a discussion about how their responses may or may not have changed. Ask questions like:
  - o What were the biggest changes, if any, to your answers? Why did your response change so much?
    - If you didn't have any changes to any of your responses, why not?
  - o How has this class changed the way you think about and participate in mathematics?
  - o What activity or lesson made the biggest impact on you and the way you think about mathematics this year? Why did it impact you so much?

Name: _____   Class Period/Subject: _____

Please fill in the following "survey" with your honest opinions about math class. I am looking forward to reading your responses.

	Strongly Disagree	Disagree	Neutral	Agree	Strongly Agree
Some people are good at math and some people are bad at math.					
I am bad at math and there is nothing I can do to change that.					
Math is unimportant to my future (college, career, parenting, etc.).					
Almost everyone I know hates math (parents, friends, etc.).					
I might like math if I was really good at it and it was easy for me.					
Math is about memorizing rules, formulas, and equations.					
I hate raising my hand or being called on because I might sound stupid if I say the wrong thing.					

My least favorite part about the math classes I have had:

I would enjoy math class more if:

It really makes me mad when my teachers:

It is hard for me to learn when other students:

Please mark YES or NO to the following questions:

Do you have regular internet access at home or somewhere nearby (library, coffee shop, etc.)?   YES   NO

Are you involved in extracurricular activities? YES NO

If yes, please list the extracurricular activities you are involved in: _____

_____

_____

Appendix C: Example Syllabus and Parent Letter

Dear Parent(s)/Guardian(s),

I would like to take this opportunity to introduce myself and to let you know what you and your student can expect from me. My name is _____ and I am your child's math teacher this year. For some of you, when I mention "math class," you are haunted by horrible memories from your schooling years. I completely understand if you cringe when you hear the words "algebra, geometry, quadratic formula," and I sympathize with you if you feel that your teachers did not do everything in their power to help you understand and appreciate the subject. I assure you, however, that I will not be like those teachers. I want to communicate to you that I genuinely care about your student and his/her success in my class. I believe that every student, regardless of their test scores, disabilities, gender, or previous failures, can succeed in learning math and I want to be a part of that for your student. In order for this to happen, I will have high expectations for your students and I will push them to grow beyond their current ability level. Below are some things that you can expect (and a few that you will not see) from my classroom.

THINGS YOU SHOULD EXPECT:
- I will have high expectations for your students. Every student has the ability to succeed in my classroom.

- I will learn the specific needs of individual students and change my instruction to meet those needs. Should you ever feel that I am not meeting those needs, please contact me as soon as possible. This includes meeting individual needs with students who have IEP's.
- I will meet your child where they are at and will help them to improve. This may mean that their level of success looks different from other students' success in the class and that is alright. I am looking to help them grow first and foremost.

THINGS YOU SHOULD NOT EXPECT:
- I will not "dumb down" the content for your students. Every student has the ability to learn at a high level and I will push your students to grow and challenge them to learn at a high level. This does NOT mean that I will go too fast for them or that I will throw things at them that they are not ready for.
- I will not accept anything but your student's best.
- I will not allow excuses like "I am just no good at math."

Please, feel free to contact me if you have any questions. Your student should allow you to read the syllabus for this class and then you may sign below stating that you have read and understand all that will be expected of your student this semester. The best way to contact me is

_____.

By signing below, I agree that I have read and understand the policies listed on the syllabus for my student's class and I agree to contact _____ if I have any questions or concerns regarding progress of my student or the above policies and procedures.

I also understand that turning in late work and having it graded are privileges that this teacher allows to help his/her students to be successful. I understand that the teacher's priority for updating grades will always be for on-time work. I understand that the teacher will do his/her best to update late work grades in a timely manner and will stress to my child that if they want their grades to be up-to-date, they should be in school and turn in their work on time.

Parent Name: _____

Student's Name: _____

Parent Email Address: _____

Phone #: _____

Preferred Method of Contact: (circle one) EMAIL   PHONE

Syllabus
TEACHER NAME AND SCHOOL YEAR
Email: TEACHER EMAIL ADDRESS

Welcome! I am excited about coming alongside you as you learn and grow mathematically. My hope for you is that you make a lot of mistakes this year in my class. Mistakes are a sign that you are learning and growing, stepping outside of your comfort zone. Mistakes show me that you have tried something new and are not afraid to take risks. We will all make mistakes, myself included. I want you to know that I am invested in your success and that I have high expectations of all of you.

Course Description:
We will begin with an introduction to fundamental concepts that are necessary for success in algebra. Following this, students will dive into linear functions, expressions of linear concepts, exponents, radicals, and polynomials. We will finish the year with an introduction to quadratic functions and equations.

Expectations:
The foundation of my classroom expectations is my belief that every student in my classroom has the following basic rights:
- Students have the right to learn in a positive and safe environment in which they will be respected, cared for, and encouraged to meet their personal needs and goals.
- Students have the right to know what is expected of them in the classroom and the consequences for their behavior.
- Students have the right to be heard by teachers and peers when communicating in a calm, polite, respectful way.

The following classroom expectations are designed to help all students receive these basic rights. I am committed to leading this classroom in a way that will ensure that students are meeting their educational needs.

Ground Rules
- Required materials that students should bring to class each day include binder, paper, pencil, textbook, calculator, homework, and any notes sheets or worksheets for the current unit. Students should use a three-ring binder to place all handouts, worksheets, and homework assignments and should bring this to each class meeting. Students should have divider tabs for their binder.
- Students are to be sitting silently in their seat with all required material when the bell rings.
- Students are to speak respectfully to other classroom members, including the teacher. Name-calling, derogatory speech, racial slurs, and cussing are not allowed.
- Students are to speak respectfully about themselves. Every student in this classroom has the potential to do well and to learn a lot and should never call themselves "stupid" or "dumb."
- Students are to respect the classroom, school property, and the belongings of others.
- Students are to listen when their peers or the teacher is talking so they can be respectful.
- The bell does not dismiss you—I dismiss you.

In general, school discipline rules will apply to this class (including dress code violations, tardiness, unexcused absences, etc.).

Discipline and Consequences:
While there will be in-class consequences for poor behavior, there are some behaviors that warrant discipline at the administrative level at the time of the offense. Continual defiance against classroom rules will result in the student entering the referral process and may require a parent meeting, a meeting with the administration, or other school-wide discipline measures.

Policies and Procedures:

Grading Policies:
Each grading period, a student's grades will be determined by daily grades/participation/homework/quizzes (50%), and tests/projects (50%). The student's overall grade for the course will be determined by equal weights for each grading period (20% each) and the final exam (20%).

Percentage	Letter Grade
100%-90%	A
89%-80%	B
79%-70%	C
69%-60%	D
0-59%	F

Late work:

- Absences must be excused in order for students to receive make-up work. A grade of zero will be entered for all unexcused absences. Students are required to turn in assignments that were due the day they were absent on the day they return. Students have the same number of days to make up their work that was assigned when they were out as days they were absent. For example, if you were absent for three days in a row, you have three school days to turn in ALL completed assignments that were assigned those three days. For extended absences due to extreme circumstances, a make-up plan can be put into effect for that student.
- Students can turn in late work for partial credit (10% off per day late, including weekends). At any time during a grading period, students can earn up to 50% credit for any missing assignment, but they must stay after school with me to make up the assignments. No late work will be accepted the last week of each grading period, and the last three weeks of the school year unless arrangements are made with me prior to these time periods.
- Turning in late work and having it graded are privileges that I allow to help my students to be successful. I want to stress that my priority for updating grades will always be for on-time work. Do not email me or ask me when your grade will be updated. If you want your grades to be up-to-date, be in school and turn in all of your work on time.
- If a student is absent when a test is scheduled or during a review session, that student shall be expected to take the test on the first day he/she returns to school following the absence. Being absent during a review day does not mean you are exempt from the test the next day.

Cell Phone Policy:

Students are not to use their cell phones in my classroom unless instructed to do so. Failure to comply with the cell phone policy will lead to "cell phone jail time". Repeated use of a cell phone or other electronic device during class time will result in the student receiving a referral.

Hall Passes:

Students are expected to take care of their personal needs between class times and during lunch as much as possible. When you need to leave the room during the class period, you will need to sign out and use a hall pass. Leaving the classroom is a privilege that can be revoked if a student abuses the privilege.

Absenteeism:

If you are absent, follow these steps:

1. Ask another student in the class what you missed from when you were absent.
2. Get any handouts given in class from the class binder.
3. Make sure you complete any assignment that was turned in during class and turn in any work or homework.

I reserve the right to change the requirements and expectations for the course and the grading criteria should it become necessary. I will give notice to students if this is the case.

For more tips and suggestions for teachers, check out my other publications on Amazon, including *10 Quick Tips for Organizing Your Classroom* and *10 Small Classroom Changes that Make a Huge Impact*, or read my blog at themrsdoering.wordpress.com.

Made in United States
North Haven, CT
30 March 2024

50667472R00032